MW00478186

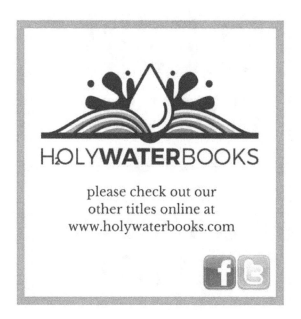

HₒLY**WATER**BOOKS

please check out our
other titles online at
www.holywaterbooks.com

BLESSED
IS HE WHO ...

MODELS OF CATHOLIC MANHOOD

By

Scott L. Smith

&

Brian J. Costello, OT, Kt HRE, OLJ

TABLE OF CONTENTS

I.

A DE-THRONED KING: FRANCESCO II, LAST KING OF BOURBON TWO SICILIES

A victim of the overwhelming transformation in European political and social life of the mid-19th century and object of scorn for generations, Francesco II, last King of Bourbon Two Sicilies, faced the reverses forced upon him with humility, piety and charity and ranks among one of the greatest Catholic gentlemen of all time.

Born January 16, 1836, Francesco II was the eldest son of King Ferdinando II and his first wife, Maria Cristina of Savoy (Blessed Queen Maria Cristina, beatified Jan. 25, 2014). His pious mother had prayed many years for the gift of an heir, particularly through the intercession of Saint Philomena, and was finally rewarded for her faith, only to die 15 days after Francesco was born.

Francesco was guided by his father and step-mother, Queen Maria Theresa, and received a strong religious and general education from the Jesuits. Unlike his father, Francesco was not trained in the military arts. His father and step-mother always inspired in him love for their kingdom, duty to its subjects, faith in the intercession of the Virgin Mary and, most of all, duty to God.

At the age of 21, Francesco requested and received the hand of 16 year-old Maria Sofia of Bavaria, daughter of Duke Maximilian and sister of Elizabeth, the wife of Emperor Franz Joseph of Austria. As she supposedly had not achieved menarche, the couple did not marry until two years later, in 1859. Only 19 days after the wedding, the illness of King of Ferdinando resulted in his death, and the young Francesco, age 23, and Sofia, 18, found themselves at the head of a vast kingdom in which internal as well as external forces had increasingly conspired to overthrow the Bourbon monarchy.

The couple reigned but one year, before the invasion of Garibaldi, supported by King Francesco's cousin Vittorio Emmanuelle of Savoy, King of Sardinia, gripped the Two Sicilies in a bloody contest. Though Francesco did not possess the military strength or political prowess of his father, he was a man of great virtue, faith, humanity and sense of duty to his subjects, especially those most in need.

Despite the threat of war and his short reign, Francesco made a number of considerable improvements in the kingdom: greater autonomy to local municipalities, abolition of duties and cutting taxes on flour by half; abolition of taxes on homes of the poor, reduction of custom duties, modernization of the incarceration system, reduction of bureaucracy, granting Palermo and Messina duty exemptions, establishment of a commercial court, diminished taxes on imported foreign goods in Catania, and granting of loans to people in need.

King Francesco also created academic chairs, high schools and colleges, and established a committee for the improvement of urban Naples. He planned for the building of government steam mills for the free milling of grain but was thwarted in this worthwhile endeavor by Garibaldi's invasion. In other areas, Francesco expanded the rail network throughout the peninsular part of the kingdom and planned to construct lines in Sicily.

A champion of public health and crop irrigation, Francesco provided public funds for the building of aqueducts, straightening of the River Sarno to create a navigable channel and continued work on cleaning the Neapolitan mashes. All of these projects were accomplished within one year.

Invasion and Exile

Giuseppe Garibaldi, at the head of the invasion of the Kingdom of the Two Sicilies, received men, ships and weapons from the Kingdom of Sardinia and money from Great Britain and France. Some of the funds were used to corrupt top Bourbon officials, who delivered entire fortresses and military posts to the greatly-outnumbered Garibaldi forces once they landed in Sicily.

The Sardinian fleet followed Garibaldi's land force bound for Naples, the capital city, while Great Britain deployed a fleet in the Gulf of Naples. Meanwhile, Sardinian General Enrico Cialdini moved towards the capital from the north, and a pitched battle was fought at Volturno.

King Vittorio Emmanuelle II of Sardinia swore friendship to his cousin, King Francesco of the Two Sicilies, and downplayed the severity the situation. Napoleon III of France publicly decried the invasion, but secretly expressed to Cavour his hopes that Nice and Savoy would be annexed to France if the French did not interfere in the Sardinian invasion.

Young King Francesco, victim of one of the largest international conspiracies of history and, above all, betrayed by his officers, government and advisers, prevented widespread bloodshed in Naples by taking refuge in the fortress of Gaeta, accompanied by Queen Sofia and their loyal troops. At Gaeta, 20,000 soldiers loyal to the Bourbon monarchy heroically resisted a savage and protracted bombardment lasting from November 13, 1860 until February 13, 1861. General Cialdini went so far as to bombard the injured Bourbonists and strafe the defenseless stretcher-bearers who attempted to extricate those hundreds buried alive in the crumbling fortress.

In addition to death by gunfire and explosions, lives among the military and the 3,000 citizens of the blockaded city were lost in an epidemic of typhus. In all, Bourbon casualties amounted to approximately 2,000 military and 200 civilian deaths and 829 soldiers wounded. By comparison, the invaders lost 46 dead and 321 wounded

Throughout the nightmare, King Francesco and Queen Sofia were of immeasurable assistance to their troops, encouraging those still fighting and consoling the injured. As food supplies dwindled, the queen often gave her own small portion to the soldiers.

After a cease-fired was effected, the King and Queen left their kingdom forever, on February 14, 1861. Soldiers and civilians alike wept uncontrollably as they knelt and clutched and kissed the hands and clothing of their unfortunate rulers. General Cialdini provided a ship on which the monarchs would depart for exile in Rome, but as a final taunt it was the one named "Garibaldi."

Francesco and Sofia hoped for a restoration to the throne, but the old Kingdom of Bourbon Two Sicilies was soon absorbed along with other smaller Italian states and the Papal States into a greater Kingdom of Italy, to be ruled by the Savoy family until 1946. For years, Bourbonists loyal to their deposed rulers and the Church made guerilla warfare upon the new Italian army and police forces, only to be mercilessly put down.

In Rome, Francesco and Sofia were hosted by Pope Pius IX, first in the Quirinale and next in the Palazzo Farnese. Earlier, when Count Cavour had proposed to divide the Papal States with him, King Francesco strongly protested through loyalty to the papacy.

Despite their misfortune, Francesco never forgot his former subjects. In 1862, within a year of his and Sofia's exile, a violent eruption of Mount Vesuvius afflicted countless residents near Naples, and Francesco responded by sending a large portion of his dwindling monetary resources for their aid.

Francesco and Maria had married in 1859, but it was nearly 11 years before they had a child. The king had a physical condition which prevented conception, but finally submitted to a surgery, and he and the queen prepared for the birth of their first born. On Christmas Eve, 1869, the Princess Maria Cristina was born while the family was in Rome. Alas, she lived but three months. Deeply grieved yet accepting God's holy will, Francesco and Sofia had no subsequent children.

Francesco and Sofia were deprived of their personal assets in the old kingdom, seized without right or justification by Garibaldi and held by the new Italian monarchy, Francesco's Savoy cousins. The former rulers moved often, living from time to time on the estates of Sofia's family in Bavaria and for a longer period in Paris. Despite reports of infidelity on the part of Sofia, Francesco would countenance neither divorce nor annulment.

Final Years

In his later years, Francesco paid extended visits to Austrian Archduke Albrecht von Habsburg at the latter's villa in Arco, then part of Austria but now part of Italy. There, Francesco, known to the populace simply as "Signore Fabiani," manifested his strongest virtues. Unknowing citizens of the town as well as intimates spoke of him as always charitable with those in need, emphasizing that no one, not even those who had plotted his earthly downfall, left his kindly presence empty-handed.

The former king of one of the most powerful nations of Europe was regularly seen arriving punctually for morning Mass in the Collegiate Church, standing composedly in line with rustic area farmers to receive his Lord in Holy Communion and to venerate relics, then partaking breakfast and reading newspapers at a nearby bar. In the afternoons, he was cordiality personified in his walks about the town and never failed to return to the church at night for communal recitation of the Rosary.

About Christmas time 1894, Francesco, a lifelong sufferer of diabetes, fell ill. Probably wishing not to draw attention to his state and alarming Archduke Albrecht, the former king moved into the Hotel Arco. As his condition worsened, he received the joy of the Last Sacraments which helped pave his way to Life Eternal.

On December 27, at the age of 58, Francesco II di Borbone, last King of Bourbon Two Sicilies, with his wife, his half-sister Maria Immacolata and the Austrian Archdukes Albrecht, Ernst and Rainier von Habsburg surrounding him, breathed his last. As he had no direct heirs, the headship of the royal house passed to his half-brother Alfonso, Count of Caserta.

Only upon his death did the citizens of snow-bound Arco learn that the cordial and devout "Signore Fabiani" who had been their pleasant neighbor was in fact King Francesco II of Bourbon Two Sicilies. Famed female journalist Matilde Serao, definitely no Bourbon supporter, spoke of him in the Naples media as the most unfortunate prince in history and lauded his virtuous life.

The Austrian military provided a troop of escort to accompany the moral remains of Francesco on a long and cold journey to Trento, where funeral services in the Church of Santa Maria del Suffragio drew most of the crowned heads of Central and Southern Europe and many Neapolitan and Sicilian nobles. On the trip from Arco to Trento and back to Arco, vast crowds turned out to line the streets and roadways and pay their final respects to a king deprived of his earthly crown but destined for an eternal one.

Francesco's remains were interred first at Schloss Arco and later removed to Rome. His widow, Sofia, died in her native Munich in 1925, aged 85, and was buried in Rome. In 1984, the two and daughter were reinterred in the Basilica of Santa Chiara in Naples, traditional last resting place of the Bourbon family.

In 2015, two religious, Don Massimo Cuofano and Don Luciano Rotolo, and layman Dr. Pantaleo Losapio organized the Fondazione Francesco II di Borbone, for the purposes of educational and charitable works and praying for the earthly glorification of King Francesco II. The Foundation has offices in Arco and Naples, and maintains a beautiful and informational internet website at: http://www.fondazionefrancescosecondo.it.

Prayer for Glorification

"O God, One and Three, from Your throne of mercy turn Your gaze upon us, and You who call us to follow Francesco II of Bourbon, having electing him King on earth, shaped his life under the Kingship of Jesus Christ crucified and risen, instilled in his heart feelings of love and patience, humility and meekness, peace and forgiveness, and clothed him of the virtues of Faith, Hope and Charity, receive our prayer and help us to walk in his footsteps and to live the virtues."

"Glorify him, please, on earth, as we believe he is already glorified in heaven, and grant that by his prayer of intercession, we can receive the graces we need. Amen."

Recite: "Our Father, Hail Mary and Glory Be"

"In accordance with the decrees of Pope Urban VIII, we declare that nothing is meant to prevent the judgment of ecclesiastical authority, and that this prayer has no purpose of public worship."

Please, should anyone receive divine graces through the intercession of King Francesco II, advise the Fondazione Francesco II di Borbone at: Viale Trento, n. 33 / b - 38068 Rovereto (TN) ITALY."

II.

A KNIGHT IN SERVICE OF CHRIST AND MARY: ARCHDUKE EUGEN OF AUSTRIA, HOCHMEISTER OF THE TEUTONIC ORDER

One of the last great figures of Catholic chivalry, Archduke Eugen von Habsburg served his Lord, Mother Mary, Church, nation and his sovereigns with admirable devotion and loyalty. Refusing to profit from the downfall of the Austro-Hungarian monarchy, he forsook the throne as well as resigned his position as the last lay-religious Hoch- und Deutschmeister of the Order of Brothers of the German House of Saint Mary in Jerusalem (the Teutonic Order).

Born May 21, 1863 at Gross-Seelowitz castle, near Brunn (Brno) in Moravia, Eugen Ferdinand Pius Bernhard Felix Maria of Austria-Teschen, Archduke of Austria and Prince of Hungary and Bohemia, was the son of Archduchess Elisabeth Franziska of Austria and her second husband and cousin, Karl Ferdinand, Archduke of Austria. His elder half-sisters were Maria Theresia, last queen of Bavaria, and Maria Christina, Queen Consort of Spain.

Eugen received a well-rounded education, delivered with strictness, which was tempered by holidays at Gmund. In Vienna, he was enrolled in the Albrechtpalais where he was taught languages, music, art history and the various military subjects. At the young age of 14, he followed family tradition and entered the military, joining the Tyrolean Kaiserjager Regiment and being commissioned lieutenant in 1877.

One year later, a month prior to his birthday, he was invested a Knight of the Golden Fleece, the first of approximately 50 military, foreign and religious honors received throughout his lifetime. He was awarded the Grand Cross of the Equestrian Order of the Holy Sepulchre in 1907.

After his service in the Kaiserjager Regiment, he transferred to a hussar regiment and participated in a number of lengthy maneuvers. In 1882, he successfully mastered an examination allowing him entrance into the Wiener Neustadt military academy. He was the only archduke to attend the two year-long course at the academy and graduated as a fully-trained officer, as opposed to other members of the royalty and nobility who were appointed solely by reason of their position.

Assigned to the General Staff in 1885, Eugen quickly rose through the ranks, commanding an infantry battalion as a lieutenant colonel, assuming command of the regiment as colonel, commanding a hussar regiment, and commanding an infantry bridge and a division in Vienna. He was appointed to the command of XIV Army Corps in Innsbruck in 1900 and promoted to General of Cavalry, commanding general in Innsbruck and defense commander for the Tyrol in the following year.

Subsequent appointments included army inspector and senior defense commander for the

Tyrol and presumptive army commander when war with Serbia seemed evident in 1909. In 1911, Eugen retired from active military service ostensibly owing to health concerns. General Conrad von Hötzendorf in his memoirs, suggested that Archduke Franz Ferdinand, Eugen's cousin and heir to the throne, had become increasingly jealous of Eugen and the latter likely retired as a way of avoiding conflict.

The Austro-Habsburg Empire was looked to in the 19th and early 20th centuries as the preeminent Catholic nation of Europe and its ruling family, the Habsburgs, the keeper of the Faith. Eugen showed a pious nature early in life and interest in theology, the latter of which culminated in his achieving a doctorate in divinity. He expressed his interest as a candidate for the Archbishopric of Olmutz and, therefore, life as a religious. Emperor Franz Josef did not concede to this desire, so in 1887, at the age of 23, the handsome and devout Eugen made his vows as a professed knight of the ancient Order of Brothers of the German House of Saint Mary in Jerusalem, popularly known as the Teutonic Order. Coincident with investiture, the emperor named Eugen coadjutor – successor - of his the latter's uncle Archduke Wilhelm, who was then Hoch- und Deutschmeister of the Order.

Upon Wilhelm's death in 1894, Eugen was installed as Hoch- und Deutschmeister and proved one of the most capable men to lead the centuries-old Order of Catholic chivalry and charity. He founded new hospitals, increased the efficiency of the Marianer (lay sisters' and brothers') nursing services and improved their training, and streamlined and expanded the Order's archives in Vienna. By 1911, the Teutonic Order numbered 20 professed knights bound as such and 30 knights of honor not bound to celibacy but who were required to furnish monetary offerings. The revenues of the Order were devoted to religious works, with administration of 50 parishes, 17 schools and nine hospitals and supported two congregations of priests and four of sisters. It performed ambulance service in time of war and paid the cost of the ambulances, for which Marianers were ambulance bearers.

When the First World War erupted over the assassination of Archduke Franz Ferdinand in 1914, Eugen immediately reported for active duty but was given a relatively minor task as patron of the volunteer war welfare organization. Four months later, he was assigned the post of commander of the forces in the Balkans, where he reorganized the badly battered 5th Army.

In 1915, Eugen was promoted to Generaloberst and assigned the command of the Southwestern Front against Italy. With his headquarters at Marburg (Maribor), his theatre stretched from the border with Switzerland to the Adriatic Sea. As the

Austro-Hungarian force faced a greatly larger Italian one, Eugen's tactic was defensive. During the First Battle of the Isonzo, he traveled back and forth along the front, participated in many conferences, streamlined supply movement to the front, appeared on the front lines and encouraged the troops, gaining great popularity. Especially endearing was his address to the troops on the birthday of Emperor Franz Josef in 1916, which may be heard in remastered format on YouTube.

In 1917, prior the attack from the South Tyrol, Eugen was named army group commander of the 11th and 3rd armies, making his headquarters at the estate of his cousin Graf von Bozen und Maurer near Bozen (Bolzano). Despite early success, the Austro-Hungarian attack had to be broken off in response to the Russians' Brusilov Offensive from the east and the resultant transfer of troops to face the Russians. Eugen had to transfer increasing numbers of his troops to the beleaguered Isonzo Army, thereby depleting himself of reserves, but he never considered withdrawal.

Eugen was promoted to Field Marshal in late 1916, and in early 1917 resumed command of the Southwest Front. Recognizing the Caporetto offensive as the last chance for victory for the Central Powers, he threw all of his energy into the task. Eugene, who was normally lenient with his troops, pushed them hard in this encounter and confusion arose in the issuance of orders.

Despite objections of the chief of the general staff, Generaloberst Baron Arz von Straussenburg, Eugen's cousin Emperor Karl (Blessed Charles of Austria) released Eugen from active service in late 1917 and the Southwestern Front command was ended. Eugen's release was made on account of the

Emperor's personal taking command and the army's offensive on the Piave.

Eugen continued to enjoy respect and admiration at war's end in 1918, and the idea of installing him as regent upon the abdication of Emperor Karl was considered. A man of high principles, Eugen, refused, as he would not accept such a position without Karl's request and blessing.

Following the war, Eugen devoted more time to the work of the Teutonic Order, charitable relief work for the war-stricken population of Austria and other works of mercy. He lived for a while in Lucerne and later in a modest hotel in Basel.

When the new government of Austria attempted to illegally seize the assets of the Teutonic Order as property of the Habsburg family in 1923, Eugen voluntarily resigned his position as Hoch- und Deutschmeister and, thereby, the Order retained its possessions. Eugen was the last hereditary grand master of the Order and it became a solely religious order of priests, brothers and sisters. The chivalric aspect of the Order was revived in 2000 under a separate Hochmeister.

In 1934, Eugen moved into the Order's home at Gumpoldskirchen near Vienna. He no longer believed in the possibility of a Habsburgs return to power, yet participated at monarchist and veterans' functions and placed himself again at the service of the Habsburg family.

Following the Anschluss of Austria in 1938, Nazi Germany under Hitler "dissolved" the Teutonic Order (as Napoleon I had done in 1809) were dissolved and its possessions confiscated. Archduke Eugene, however, held the admiration of both the Axis and Allied powers. Likely due to intervention by Hermann Göring and other senior Nazi military figures, he survived the Second World War in a rented house at Hietzing. In 1945, Eugen returned to the Tyrol and received through the French occupying forces a small rental villa at Igls.

On May 21, 1953, the whole of the city of Innsbruck and much of Catholic Europe celebrated Archduke Eugen's 90th birthday. He lived for more than a year longer, dying on December 30, 1954, in the Teutonic Order house at Meran, surrounded by the brothers of the Order from Lana.

The funeral services in Innsbruck on January 6, 1955 witnessed widespread mourning and tributes, with massed thousands defying cold weather to line the route of the cortege. Eugen was buried in St. Jakobskirche, next to Archduke Maximilian III (1558–1619), and there awaits the Second Coming of the Lord he valiantly served.

III.

AN ATTORNEY AND HUSBAND: BLESSED LUIGI BELTRAME QUATTROCCHI

On October 21, 2001, an estimated 50,000 men, women and children defied threatening weather to crowd St. Peter Basilica and Square in Rome as Pope John Paul II declared as "Blessed" Luigi and Maria Beltrame Quattrocchi, the first beatified married couple of the Church. To the assembly, the Holy Father stated:

> Maria and Luigi were beatified as a married couple. They are not 'clerics or religious.' They are lay people and they are married with children. They symbolize all married couples who have lived and still live today in their married life 'the holiness' which is the call of all Christians....

> Drawing on the word of God and the witness of the saints, the blessed couple lived an ordinary life in an extraordinary way. Among the joys and anxieties of a normal family, they knew how to live an extraordinarily rich spiritual life....

A Family is Formed

Born in Catania, Sicily in 1880, Luigi Beltrame was adopted at age 11 by his childless uncle Luigi Quattrocchi and wife, for which the young man added "Quattrocchi" to his surname. He received a law degree from La Sapienza university in Rome and worked as an attorney for the Inland Revenue department. Blessed Luigi's children related that their father was always a man of great honesty and integrity but his faith was not exceptionally strong in his earliest years. After meeting Maria Luisa Corsini at her family's home in Florence, however, Luigi's interior life took a decided turn.

Maria, born 1884 to one of Italy's most illustrious princely families, was erudite and urbane but also deeply spiritual. Her collateral ancestors included St. Andrew Corsini, Pope Clement XII (born Lorenzo Corsini) and three Corsini Cardinals, in addition to Roman Princes, Counts Palatine and Grandees of Spain. A lover of peace, sensitive Maria, as a child, would place a small olive leaf under her parents' napkins at table to express her desire that her short-tempered military father and domineering mother would not quarrel.

Once they met, the attraction between Maria and Luigi was immediate, as they both enjoyed literature, music, theatre, the beauty of nature and travel. When Luigi fell gravely ill in late 1904, Maria was greatly distressed and sent him an image of the Madonna of Pompeii. This event revealed to the two young people the depth of their love for each other, and they were married on November 25, 1905 in the Basilica di Santa Maria Maggiore in Rome.

As their marriage progressed, Luigi grew in faith. He and Maria attended daily morning Mass together, and Luigi charmingly reserved his "Good morning!" greeting to her until after the service, as if to acknowledge that only then, after the Sacred Liturgy shared together, did their day truly begin.

Within four years of marriage, Luigi and Maria Beltrame Quattrocchi were blessed with three healthy children: Filippo, born in 1906, Stefania , and Cesare, in a difficult labor in 1909. Maria's fourth pregnancy was life-threatening and gynecologists advised Maria and Luigi to abort the child. The Quattrocchis, gazing intently upon the doctors' crucifix, adamantly refused an abortion and placed all their trust in God and the Virgin Mary.

Maria endured dangerous hemorrhages and was bedridden for four months, and their daughter Stefania later recalled Luigi weeping as he spoke to a priest in church during that trying period. After an induced labor in the eighth month, Maria courageously gave birth to their fourth child and second daughter, Enrichetta, in 1914. One of the couple's first acts was to thank God.

Living "From the Roof Up"
In her moving work *Radiography of a Marriage* (1952), Maria wrote: "Since the birth of our first son, we began dedicating ourselves to the children, forgetting ourselves.... In order to love our

children more, we tried to better ourselves by correcting our shortcomings and improving our characters.... We both felt the tremendous responsibility in front of God, Who had entrusted the children to our care and of our country that expected loving citizens.... Educating children is the 'art of all arts' and brings along serious difficulties. But one thing is certain: as two bodies in one, we both aimed at their best, ready to avoid everything that could harm them; this implied some personal sacrifices. The joy of dedication to our children compensated everything, because that joy was God's joy."

Family life was never dull in the Quattrocchi home in the Via Depretis in Rome. Relatives and friends recall the "noisy joy" which characterized the Quattrocchis, especially at mealtime. The family enjoyed sports and trips to the seashore and mountains. In 1928, Luigi and Maria acquired property at Serravalle on which they built a house, complete with small chapel where, by special permission, they were able to enshrine the Blessed Sacrament.

In addition to Luigi's legal profession and Maria's career as a professor and catechist and her publication of many works on education and family life, the Quattrocchis were members of The Third Order Regulars of St. Francis of Penance, involved in various marriage and family apostolates and service to the poor youth of Rome. They founded the Associazione Scouts Cattolici Italiani, the Italian scout organization; the Azione Cattolica, the largest Catholic lay organization in Italy; and UNITALSI, an association which coordinates pilgrimages of the infirm to Loretto and Lourdes. The Quattrocchi sons were Scouts in their youth and, after their ordinations, served as Scout chaplains.

Luigi and Maria earnestly reared their four children to love and live the spiritual life. They often told friends and relatives that they wanted their children to appreciate life "from the roof up," that is, concentrating on Heaven. For more than 20 years, the Quattrocchis received spiritual direction from two renowned prelates, Father Pellegrino Paoli and Father Matheo Crawley. The family, led by Luigi, prayed the Rosary together each evening after dinner, and the image of the Sacred Heart of Jesus solemnly enthroned by Father Crawley held the place of honor on the dining room mantel.

The Quattrocchis held a family holy hour on the eve of the First Friday of each month, practiced night vigil prayer, attended weekend retreats and pursued graduate courses in spirituality. Luigi's profound devotion before the Blessed Sacrament and his love of assisting visiting priests celebrate Mass in the family home were remembered with great emotion by his children.

For the Quattrocchis, the home was a "little Bethany" where love for one another in God reigned supreme. Maria was renowned for her hospitality and here her spirituality was evident, in that gossip, resentment and bitterness were banned.

Youngest daughter Enrichetta stated that her parents were, obviously, not immune to disagreements between themselves but they never allowed the children to witness such. Luigi and Maria solved problems through discussion and always displayed a spirit of harmony and unity. Luigi's intuition of Maria's concerns was proverbial. Once, on a business trip away from Rome, he stopped in Naples to telegraph Maria, saying he knew exactly what she wished to discuss with him.

Younger son Cesare recalled of family life: "There was always a supernatural, serene, and happy atmosphere in our home, but not excessively pious. No matter what the issues facing us, they always resolved it by saying that it had to be appealed 'to Heaven'."

Filippo, the older son, stated: "The aspect that characterized our family life was the atmosphere of normality that our parents created in the constant seeking of transcendental values."

Three of the four Quattrocchi children chose religious vocations: Filippo became Rev. Tarcisio, a diocesan priest, and Cesare entered the Trappist order of Brothers and became Rev. Paolino. Their sister Stefania recalled: "When the two boys left the house, it left a huge emptiness. Papa was the one who felt it the most, to the point of physical illness." However, this grief passed, and Maria later wrote to her sons: "Thinking of you is for me, after the Mass and Communion, my only rest, the single radiant refuge in my soul blessing the Lord."

In 1927, Stefania entered the Benedictine convent in Milan and took the name Sister Maria Cecilia. The youngest Quattrocchi - Enrichetta – recalled: "My sister's departure made a violent tear in Papa's heart. I can still see, more than 70 years later, the silent, discrete tears of my father on his knees, while on the other side of the grille, the ceremony of his daughter's taking of the habit took place."

Enrichetta, for whom all of the family had prayed so fervently during Maria's difficult fourth pregnancy, selflessly lived the Fourth Commandment in dedicating herself to the care of her parents throughout their remaining years.

During World War II, both of the Quattrocchi sons served as chaplains in the Italian Army. Maria, who had served as a volunteer nurse during the Ethiopian War, served again in this capacity. Their home in the Via Depretis was a beacon of faith and charity during the frightful German occupation of Rome. No one suffering from the effects of the occupation and knocking at the Quattrocchis' door was ever turned away or refused food. Their home ever remained open to refugees, including Jews, for whom they went to heroic lengths and would have suffered terrible consequences if detected by the German authorities.

Home to God, and Beatification

As they aged, Luigi and Maria devoted even more time to prayer and contemplation within their home, becoming an example of piety to all who knew them. In 1951, Luigi, Maria, and the inseparable Enrichetta spent a last, beautiful day together in the mountains, shortly after which Luigi died of a heart attack at the age of 71. By the grace of God, all three of the Quattrocchi children in religious life happened to be in Rome at the time and the entire family was able to attend Mass and re-consecrate as a family to the Sacred Heart of Jesus shortly before Luigi died.

Luigi Beltrame Quattrocchi was remembered by many as a man of great ability, integrity and virtue, who never spoke of the many professional honors awarded him and who refused positions of higher authority if he felt that they would, in any way, compromise his first duties to God and family.

Standing before Luigi's mortal remains, a formerly atheistic colleague told the Quattrocchi sons: "You see, during all the years that we worked together, your father never pestered me with sermons. But I want to tell you, it's through his life that I discovered God and that I love the Gospel. Pray for me!"

Maria, heartbroken by Luigi's passing, was able to write a few months later: "Luigi is always and incessantly the love and inconsolable sorrow of each and all of us, yet he helps us, he is near to us, and he loves us as much and even more, if it is possible, than before. Little by little, he is present to me ever more, most of all, at Communion, before the altar. "

Though gradually reducing her external work, Maria continued a life of prayer and writing on behalf of couples, families and children. She died in 1965, having just recited the noon Angelus, in the arms of Enrichetta, the child for whom she had been willing to sacrifice her life.

The elder Quattrocchi daughter, Sister Maria Cecilia (born Stefania), died in 1993. In November of the following year, the beatification cause of Luigi and Maria Beltrame Quattrocchi was opened. Pope John Paul II decided that a miracle – the cure of bone alterations of Italian neurosurgeon Gilberto Grossi – was due to the intercession of Luigi and

Maria Beltrame Quattrocchi. The couple's three surviving children – Father Tarcisio, Father Paolino and Signorella Enrichetta - had the joy of living to witnessing their parents' beatification.

Many observers noted that the time for the beatification of Luigi and Maria Beltrame Quattrocchi was providential, occurring as it did shortly after the tragic events of 9-11 in New York City, when families around the world were stunned by the ever present and unpredictable threat of terrorism.

The earthly remains of Blessed Luigi and Maria Beltrame Quattrocchi are entombed in the crypt of the Sanctuario della Madonna del Divono Amore (Sanctuary of Our Lady of Divine Love) in suburban Rome. Countless pilgrims visit the sanctuary to pay their respects to and draw inspiration from the blessed couple, particularly on their feast day – November 25 – which is their wedding anniversary. A chapel within the sanctuary is one of the most popular European wedding venues.

The Quattrocchis' "miracle child" – Enrichetta - lived to age 98, dying in 2012. She had the joy of helping others see in her blessed parents an example of living a life of faith, service and devotion. She was named Honorary President of the Associazione Beati Coniugi Maria e Luigi Beltrame Quattrocchi, abbreviated A.MAR.LUI, upon its founding at Pescara, Italy in 2010. The goals of this organization include: conjugal unity and respect for each other's vocations; active service to family, society and Church; embracing all people, in particular engaged and married couples, in their unique situations; a commitment to learn from everyone in a spirit of universal brotherhood; and promotion of Christian love, respect for the differences of others, harmony among spouses, the educational task of parents and a spirit of filial gratitude.

For more information, see the A.MAR.LUI website at: www.luigiemaria.com.

IV.

AN ATHLETE: BLESSED PIER GIORGIO FRASSATTI

In this trying time that our country is going through, we Catholics and especially we students, have a serious duty to fulfill: our self-formation....

I urge you with all the strength of my soul to approach the Eucharistic Table as often as possible. Feed on this Bread of the Angels from which you will draw the strength to fight inner struggles....

When God is with us, we do not need to be afraid. (Pier Giorgio Frassati)

Blessed Pier Giorgio Frassati, the "Saint for the Youth of the Third Millennium," lived life to the fullest, enjoying sports and the companionship of people of all ages, and manifesting his deep love for Christ with selfless service to the needy and a mission to sanctify society and politics.

Pier Giorgio was born in Turin, Italy on Holy Saturday, April 6, 1901. His father, Alfredo Frassati, was the founder and director of the liberal newspaper *La Stampa* and a leader in Italian politics, serving as senator and later as Italy's ambassador to Germany. Pier Giorgio's mother, nee Adelaide Amentis, was a painter and socialite. Pier

Giorgio's life and work transpired between two devastating World Wars, when his country was in social and political turmoil and with Fascism on the rise.

Pier Giorgio's parents were Catholics in name only, he father being described as an agnostic, and their marriage was an unhappy, often rancorous one. By the grace of God, Pier Giorgio developed a deep spiritual life in his childhood, particularly in Adoration of the Blessed Sacrament, praying the Rosary and giving all he could of himself and his resources to those in need. He remained with his parents throughout his life, hoping to lessen the tension between them and keeping the family intact. Heartbroken, Pier Giorgio even sacrificed his love for a young Spanish lady, Laura Hidalgo, whom his parents considered below their social status.

In 1918 Pier Giorgio joined the St. Vincent de Paul Society and dedicated much of his spare time between studies to serving the sick and needy. Pier Giorgio did not have a religious calling but wanted to serve God and society as a lay person. He decided upon the career of mining engineer so he could "serve Christ better among the miners." In 1919, he joined the Catholic Student Federation and the Popular Party, a political organization promoting the Catholic Church's teachings. He also helped establish a Catholic daily newspaper, *Momento*, based on the principles of Pope Leo XIII's encyclical on social and economic matters, Rerum Novarum.

Although the Frassati family was wealthy, the father was frugal and never gave his two children, Pier Giorgio and his older sister, Luciana, much spending money. What little he did receive, however, Pier Giorgio gave to help the poor, even giving his streetcar fare to those in need and then running home from classes or spiritual work to be on time for meals in a house where punctuality and frugality were the law. When asked by friends why he often rode third class on the trains he would reply with a smile, "Because there is not a fourth class." He wanted to identify with the poor in everything he did.

One day when Pier Giorgio was a child, a poor mother and son came begging to the Frassati home. Pier Giorgio answered the door and, seeing the boy barefoot, promptly removed his own shoes and gave them to the boy. At Pier Giorgio's graduation, his father gave him the choice of money or a car; he chose the money and gave it to the poor. He obtained a room for a poor elderly woman evicted from her tenement, provided a bed for a consumptive invalid and supported the family of a sick and grieving widow. He kept a little ledger containing detailed accounts of his transactions, and while he lay on his death bed, he gave instructions to his sister, Luciana, asking her to see to the needs of families who depended on his charity. He even took the time, with a near-paralyzed hand, to write a note to a friend in the St. Vincent de Paul Society with instructions regarding their weekly Friday visits to impoverished families.

Only Pier Giorgio's beneficiaries and God knew of his selfless charity work and personal sacrifices; he never mentioned it to others.

One night while with his family in Berlin, with the temperature at 12 degrees below zero, Pier Giorgio literally gave his overcoat to a poor old man shivering with cold. His father scolded him, and he replied simply: 'But you see, Papa, it was cold.'"

Pier Giorgio's parents considered him undisciplined, a hopeless student with little future. They could not understand why he prayed the Rosary so frequently, attended Mass and received Holy Communion every day and attended night-long Adoration of the Blessed Sacrament. They did all they could to emotionally deter him from his active Catholicism. Pier Giorgio remained unbroken in his faith and work, and yet was always the loving son.

Verso l'alto
Pier Giorgio Frassati

In between his studies, devotions and charitable work, handsome and vigorous Pier Giorgio spent time in the countryside with friends, mountain climbing and snow skiing being his favorite sports. On these outings, the young friends - who humorously called themselves "The Sinister Ones" – enjoyed hours of fun and laughter but likewise shared their religious inspirations and spiritual lives. Pier Giorgio's famous motto, "Verso l'alto,"

Italian for "To the heights," meant reaching for God as well as the mountain peaks. His regular habit was to attend Mass before heading to the mountains and of visiting the Blessed Sacrament upon his return. "If my studies permitted, I would spend whole days on the mountains, admiring in that pure atmosphere the magnificence of God," he said.

Pier Giorgio also enjoyed the theatre, opera and museum visits. He loved art and music, could quote entire sections of Dante and other classical writings. Though without a fine voice, he sung both religious and classical tunes with gusto and conviction.

Fear never deterred Pier Giorgio Frassati from expressing and promoting his faith in Christ. In a Church-sponsored rally in Rome, he withstood police violence and encouraged the other young people by grabbing the banner which the police had knocked out of someone's hands. Pier Giorgio held it even higher and used the pole to block the blows. When the students were arrested, he refused special treatment that he might have received because of his father's political position, preferring to stay with his friends. On another occasion, some Fascists broke into his family's home at night to attack him and his father. Pier Giorgio beat them off and chased them down the street single-handedly.

In late June 1925, Pier Giorgio was afflicted by an acute attack of polio which doctors later speculated he contracted from the poor and sick that he tended. Neglecting his own health because his grandmother was dying, Pier Giorgio's illness became too advanced for treatment. His parents only realized his suffering when it was too late. Through days of terrible and paralyzing pain, he never complained and prayed as long as he had the strength. On her part, his mother denied his friends' and even the Archbishop of Turin's requests to visit and comfort him. Thus deprived but ever gracious, Pier Giorgio Frassati returned his soul to the Lord he so loved on July 4, 1925. He was only 24.

The Frassatis expected their great political and social friends and some of Pier Giorgio's circle to offer their condolences and attend the funeral. They were dumbfounded, however, when a steady stream of people totally unknown to them visited their home to pray beside Pier Giorgio's remains, at the lines of kneeling people outside, at the streets of Turin crowded with thousands of weeping and praying people, particularly the poor, who pushed toward the unadorned coffin as it was borne to the parish church of La Crocetta.

Most of the poor, too, had a surprise as they learned that the young man who had given to and served them so faithfully and generously was from such a rich and influential family. It was these poor people who petitioned the Archbishop of Turin to begin the cause for Pier Giorgio's canonization. The process was opened in 1932 and he was beatified on May 20, 1990 by Pope John Paul II. Blessed Pier Giorgio Frassati's feast day is July 4 – the day of his death - and his body, miraculously incorrupt 88 years after his death, lies in a chapel of Turin Cathedral.

Devotion to the intercession of Blessed Giorgio and advocacy of his ideals is practiced by countless people, particularly school students and young adults, the world over. The prime proponents of the Frassati message are the Associazione Beati Pier Giorgio Frassati in Rome and FrassatiUSA in this country. Detailed information on their work may be found online as well as that of Frassati Groups which have developed spontaneously across the United States in honor and emulation of Blessed Pier Giorgio Frassati, an athlete for Christ, a man of the Beatitudes and a Catholic Gentleman par excellence.

V.

A HEALER: FRANCIS XAVIER SEELOS, C.Ss.R.

Soon, the New Orleans Saints might be adding one more to their number. Blessed Francis Xavier Seelos is gaining plenty of popularity, and not just here in Louisiana. His cause for canonization should have several miraculous healings from which to choose. Miracles seem to be pouring out of his National Shrine on Josephine Street in New Orleans. The shrine, its museum, and St. Mary of the Assumption church are all worth a visit, *especially* if you or someone you know is in need of a miracle.

The life of Father Seelos, as he's most often called, was full of amazing historical confluences for such a uniquely humble man, including encounters with other saints and even President Lincoln. His final days, too, were remarkable for the palpable taste of heaven on earth, an experience which captured the attention of the entire city of New Orleans.

I've also included his intercessory prayer at the end. Make sure you learn about this remarkable man, so he can intercede for you as he has for so many others!

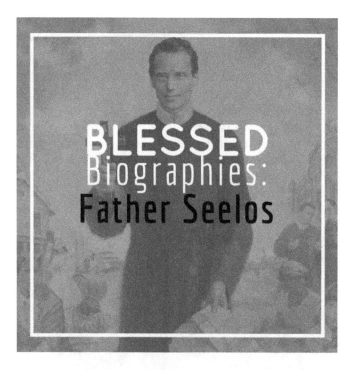

BLESSED Biographies: Father Seelos

Francis Xavier Seelos was born and baptized on January 11, 1819 in Fussen, Germany. During the celebration of Christmas which immediately preceded his birth, in a small chapel elsewhere in Germany, one of the most beloved carols of all time was performed for the very first time. Seelos was thus born alongside "Silent Night."

Seelos' childhood home of Fussen is known for the picturesque Neuschwanstein castle, but also for the Benedectine Monastery of St. Mang or St. Magnus, who is also the city's patron saint. Not only was Seelos' boyhood parish church named for St. Magnus, his father also bore the name.

It is interesting that Seelos would later be invoked for the healing of *humans*, because his boyhood patron, St. Magnus, has long been invoked for the healing of animals, especially cattle - not to mention protection from snake bites! Perhaps St. Magnus kept a watchful eye on Seelos, even after the young priest moved to the New World.

Seelos, for his part, had his eye on the priesthood from a very young age and entered seminary in 1842. He originally entered as a diocesan priest, but God had plans for him beyond the Diocese of Augsburg. Soon after entering seminary, Seelos met the missionaries of the Congregation of the Most Holy Redeemer, known as the "Redemptorists."

The Redemptorists were founded by Saint Alphonsus Liguori, whom Saint Pope John Paul II called "a missionary who went in search of the most abandoned souls." Like Liguori, the Redemptorists are the shepherds of the most lost of the world's lost sheep. Thus, Seelos came to minister to the German-speaking immigrants to the United States.

THE NEW WORLD

Sailing from Le Havre, France, Seelos arrived in New York City on April 20, 1843. He would be followed by over six million more German immigrants over the next half century. German-speaking priests were already in desperate supply. In 1836, when Seelos' fellow German and Redemptorist, Saint John Neumann, arrived in New York City, there were only three German-speaking priests in the entire Diocese of New York City. In the 1840s, German-speaking districts would pop up in cities across America. With each new district, a new Catholic church would spring up, requiring thousands more German-American priests.

Two Christmases later on December 22, 1844, Seelos was ordained a priest in Baltimore, Maryland at the Redemptorist Church of St. James. Soon thereafter, he was moved to St. Philomena parish in Pittsburgh. There, an amazing historical confluence occurred. He served as the assistant pastor to (another) great saint, Saint John Neumann. Regarding their relationship, Seelos said: "He has introduced me to the active life" and "guided me as a spiritual director and confessor."

Even in proximity to the great Saint John Neumann, Seelos' fame began to spread. His growing skills as a spiritual director and pastor while in Pittsburgh have been elsewhere described:

His availability and innate kindness in understanding and responding to the needs of the faithful quickly made him well known as an expert confessor and spiritual director, so much so that people came to him even from neighboring towns.

In fact, even though many years would pass since he had moved from Pittsburgh, it would be here that rumor would begin to spread of his miraculous intercession following his death.

Faithful to the Redemptorist charism, Seelos practiced a simple lifestyle. He may have been describing his own daily routine when giving the following advice for a spiritual regime:

In the morning, get up at five o'clock; in the evening to bed at ten. Daily, if possible, attend Mass, and in the afternoon a visit to the Blessed Sacrament if there is some free time at your disposal. Every day try to say five decades of the Rosary. During your work see in your mind one or the other of the Stations of the Cross and then, in spirit, make personal applications about the mystery meditated upon. At the beginning take one Station to which you ordinarily have a great devotion and gradually you will be in condition to visit, one by one, all the fourteen Stations in a spirit of contemplation during your work and to make practical applications in your heart.[1]

Seelos was especially concerned with the instruction of little children in the faith. Not only did he have a special tenderness for children, but he viewed their proper instruction as critical to the growth of the Christian community. His simple manner of preaching would have reached children, as well as adults. His preaching, always rich in Biblical content, was understood by everyone, regardless of education, culture, or background. His confessional, too, was visited by all. He once wrote, "I hear confessions in German, English, French, of Whites and of Blacks."[2]

THE PAULINE PERIOD, SEELOS' MISSIONARY JOURNEYS

In 1854, Father Seelos was transferred from Pittsburgh back to Baltimore. He would never again spend so much time in one place. The American Redemptorists recognized Seelos' special gift for teaching and training youth by naming him as the Prefect of Students. Above all, Seelos "strove to instill in these future Redemptorist missionaries the enthusiasm, the spirit of sacrifice, and apostolic zeal for the spiritual and temporal welfare of the people." [3]

Pittsburgh would try to reclaim Seelos, and such as their Bishop. In 1860 on the eve of the Civil War, the Bishop of Pittsburgh, Michael O'Connor recommended Seelos as the man most qualified to succeed him. Seelos wrote Pope Paul IX explaining his inadequacy and pleading "to be liberated from this calamity." [4] The pope ultimately did excuse him from this responsibility. This would begin something of a Pauline period of missionary journeys for the Redemptorist priest.

In the succeeding years, Seelos dedicated himself to the life of an itinerant missionary crisscrossing America and preaching in English and German. He would spend time in Connecticut, Illinois, Michigan, Missouri, New Jersey, New York, Ohio, Pennsylvania, Rhode Island, and Wisconsin.

At the peak of the Civil War, the U.S. government enacted new draft laws requiring every able-bodied male to make himself available for military duty. Discontent over the draft boiled over in the New York City draft riots, the largest insurrection in American history. President Lincoln was forced to divert troops fresh from the Battle of Gettysburg to restore order to the city. Seelos, then Superior of the Redemptorist seminary, traveled to Washington to intercede before Lincoln himself and plead for an exemption from military service for the seminarians. This would mark another extraordinary historical convergence in the life of this remarkable priest. Lincoln, according to Seelos' own account, was extremely receptive to the priest's prayer and promised to do all in his power to answer it. Throughout the remainder of the war, none of Seelos' students were drafted.

NEW ORLEANS

Father Seelos received his final assignment in 1866, while briefly serving as a parish priest in Detroit. His time in New Orleans, at least in life, would also prove short. He embarked for Louisiana by train after making a ten-day retreat and general confession at St. Michael's in Chicago. His Redemptorist brothers there recounted that Father Seelos left for Louisiana having clearly seen in advance what awaited him there and knowing he would never see them again.[6]

Seelos must have received a very specific vision of the remainder of his life indeed, based on the account of two School Sisters of Notre Dame who he met aboard the train. When they inquired as to the length of his stay in New Orleans, he remarked that he would remain in New Orleans for a year and then die of yellow fever.

In New Orleans, Seelos served as pastor of the Redemptorist church of St. Mary of the Assumption, which is now home to the National

Shrine of Blessed Selos. There, he was known as being "joyously available to his faithful and singularly concerned for the poorest and the most abandoned."

The *Redemptorist Community Chronicle* includes an account of Father Seelos being passed the reins of Superior over the large community of priests and students in New Orleans. According to the *Chronicle*, he more closely resembled a novice than the well-traveled and accomplished priest he was, because he was "more desirous of being led than leading." His example "confounded" his brothers, calling them to a place where they became "humbler and more Redemptorist" than before. According to Father Benedict Neithart, C.Ss.R., Seelos was generally regarded by all the members of the community as a "living Saint."

True to the model established by Saint Alphonsus Liguori, after a life of serving the "most abandoned", Father Seelos dedicated himself to caring for the victims of yellow fever, as well as his many other duties. Father Neithart recounts never once seeing Seelos idle during his final year and "literally killing himself with labor, mortification, and exertion, but nevertheless [being] the most cheerful and humorous of the community."

Epidemics of yellow fever had been plaguing the port city since just before Seelos' birth. In 1867 alone, over three thousand people would succumb to the illness in New Orleans.[7] The total number of yellow fever victims in 1867 - 3,107 - would include at least one future saint and martyr. In September of that year, exhausted from endless hours of visiting and caring for the sick, Seelos contracted the disease.

For several weeks, he patiently endured his illness and received a constant stream of visitors. During this time, Seelos is also reported to have placed his hand to his heart and said, "I feel like I have traveled enough. I shall never leave New Orleans."[8]

He continued to receive people for the Sacrament of Confession even when, because of the advance of the fever, he struggled to remember the words of absolution and even to breathe. Nevertheless, a pleasant smile and cheer never left his face. His brothers reported that the change in his color clearly indicated the degree of his sufferings:

> He had not merely turned yellow from jaundice, but brown like a Spaniard. No one could look at him for a long time without being moved to tears with pity.

Masses were being said almost constantly for Father Seelos' recovery, and even the New Orleans newspapers carried a daily update of Seelos' health. Doctors attributed the final days of his life to a miracle. In these final days, two of his brother priests, including the Father-Rector of the community, came to his bedside with knee injuries and asked for healing. Both were immediately cured.

When death appeared close at hand on Wednesday, October 2, Seelos expressed his lifelong desire to die on a Friday, as Jesus had. Father Seelos miraculously endured another two days and passed on to eternal life on Friday, October 4, 1867, the Feast of Saint Francis of Assisi, at the age of 48.

His Holiness Pope John Paul II, proclaimed Father Seelos "Blessed" in St. Peter's Square on

April 9th of the Solemn Jubilee Year 2000. His Feast Day is celebrated on October 5.

PRAYER FOR THE INTERCESSION OF BLESSED F. X. SEELOS

O my God, I truly believe Thou art present with me. I adore Thy limitless perfections. I thank Thee for the graces and gifts Thou hast given to Father Seelos. If it is Thy holy will, please let him be declared a saint of the Church so that others may know and imitate his holy life. Through his prayers please give me this favor [here mention your special intention].

[1] Hoegerl, Carl W., editor and translator. *Sincerely Seelos: The Collected Letters of Blessed Francis Xavier Seelos* (New Orleans: The Redemptorists/Seelos Center, 2008).

[2-5] From the Homily of the Holy Father, as adapted by cssr.news and seelos.org.

[7] George Augustin, *History of Yellow Fever* (New Orleans, 1909), as referenced by nutrias.org/facts/feverdeaths.htm.

[6,8] *Death, Where Is Your Sting?*, The quotes from this section come from a tender account of Seelos' final weeks of life as told primarily by those who witnessed his death. Seldom-revealed details of his encounter with yellow fever transport us to the bedside of a true martyr. Hardcover, 175 pp., photos. Available at the Seelos Shrine gift shop.

VI.

A COMPUTER NERD: CARLO ACUTIS, SERVANT OF GOD

T here's a path to holiness that has worked over and over. It's the same path that allowed Saint Thérèse of Lisieux to become a Saint and Doctor of the Church, despite having lived only to the age of 24.

You never know how many years you'll have, so the time is always NOW to become a Saint.

So what is the quickest, surest path to Heaven and Sainthood? It's the same path that Carlo Acutis, Servant of God, took in his short life.

Despite his short life, Carlo Acutis brought the Gospel to entirely new places and into entirely new forms. For this, he may one day be called the Patron Saint of the Internet and possibly even social media.

What was Carlo's secret? It was what he chose to be the single goal and objective of his short life.

BLESSED
Biographies:
Carlo Acutis

Read below to find out more about this young man's incredible, albeit short, life:

BORN TO A LUKEWARM FAMILY

Not too long ago, it seems, Carlo Acutis was born in London on May 3, 1991. His parents, Andrea and Antonia, were there on business. They returned home to Milan in September.

"Madame, your son is special!" Carlo's mother often heard this remark from the parish priest, teachers, classmates, and even the porter of their building on Via Ariosto, where they moved in 1994.

The boy's exceptional qualities were due to a very special friendship. Out of nowhere it seemed, as Carlo's family did not assiduously attend church, Carlo developed a great friendship with Jesus.

Carlo's mother, Antonia Acutis, recalls how little Carlo could not pass in front of a church without asking to go in and greet Jesus. She was surprised to discover her son reading saint biographies and the Bible, and even more surprised when her son began asking questions of such depth and profundity that she was unable to answer:

> I was perplexed by his devotion. He was so small and so sure. I understood that it was his thing, but that he was also calling me. So I began my journey of rapprochement with faith. I followed him.

At the age of seven and quite on his own, Charles asked to receive First Holy Communion. After questioning the precocious boy, Monsignor Pasquale Macchi guaranteed his maturity and level of Christian formation. However, he made a single recommendation: the celebration should take place in a place free from distractions. As such, on June 16, 1998, Carlo received the Eucharist in silence of the Bernaga monastery, near Lecco.

"As a little boy, especially after his First Communion, he never missed his daily appointment with the Holy Mass and the Rosary, followed by a moment of Eucharistic adoration," recalls Carlo's mother.

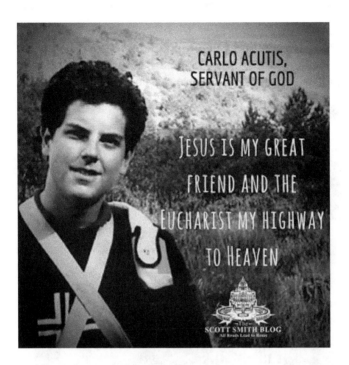

CARLO ACUTIS, SERVANT OF GOD

JESUS IS MY GREAT FRIEND AND THE EUCHARIST MY HIGHWAY TO HEAVEN

SCOTT SMITH BLOG
All Roads Lead to Rome

UNITED TO THE EUCHARIST FROM A YOUNG AGE

Carlo first attended school with the Marcelline Sisters. He received his secondary education at the hands of the Jesuits at the Leo XIII Classical Lyceum. The Classical Lyceum is the oldest form of public secondary school in Italy, as well as the most rigorous. The *Liceo classico* was for a time the only path to university-level studies.

Carlo thrived in this environment, becoming a young, affectionate and brilliant young man.

Ever since boyhood and especially following that First Communion, Carlo's life revolved around a fixed point: daily Mass. "The Eucharist," he said, "is my highway to Heaven." He also frequently received the Sacrament of Reconciliation. As an adolescent, he added to his spiritual regimen a Daily Rosary and Eucharistic Adoration.

He spoke thus of Eucharistic Adoration: "If we get in front of the sun, we get sun tans ... but when we get in front of Jesus in the Eucharist, we become Saints."

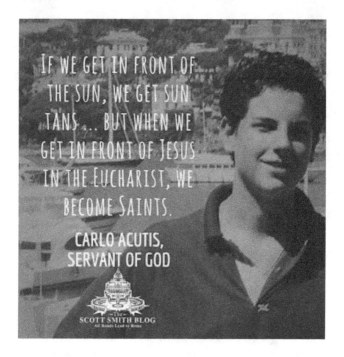

But how does even a Saint survive high school these days? And with holiness intact?

A SAINT IN HIGH SCHOOL?

Carlo was convinced that he would not grow old. "I will die young," he often repeated. This is perhaps why he filled his days with such a whirlwind of activity, teaching the boys from the catechism, feeding the poor at the Caritas cafeteria, and spending time with the children of the oratory.

While still achieving excellent grades in high school and between all his charity work, Carlo still found time to play the saxophone, play football, design computer programs, and, like any other red-blooded teenager, play video games.

He was naturally inclined toward computer science and was even considered brilliant by practicing engineers who encountered his technical intuition and savvy. Carlo's interests ranged from computer programming to editing films, from creating websites to writing periodicals.

His classmates looked to him, not only for advice or help, but also because of his way of putting people at ease. Carlo seemed to have a way with people from all backgrounds.

Carlo's friendly face was a common sight in his neighborhood. He befriended everybody, including the gatekeepers, janitors, and other domestic servants that worked in his neighborhood. These workers were often non-Europeans with Muslim and Hindu backgrounds. Carlo told everybody about his love for Christ, and people couldn't help but listen and share in his joy. One such domestic worker was Rajesh, a Hindu and Brahmin. A friendship developed between Rajesh and Carlo. The friendship was of such a profound nature that Rajesh converted to Catholicism.

This is what Rajesh had to say about his friend, Carlo:

> He told me that I would have been happier if I had approached Jesus. I was baptized Christian because it was he who so affected me with his profound faith, his charity, and his purity. I have always considered it out of the ordinary because a boy so young, so

handsome, and so rich, normally prefers to have a different life.

Speaking of Carlo's affluence, he was careful never to waste money. He was known to donate sleeping bags to the homeless on his way to Mass in Santa Maria Segreta. He also donated to the Capuchins of Viale Piave for the service of meals to the homeless.

Carlo never hid what made him most happy ...

Carlo was always inviting his friends to go with him to Mass. For his friends to become reconciled to God, this was the source of his joy. Carlo wrote the following in his journal:

Sadness is the gaze turned towards oneself, happiness is the gaze turned towards God. Conversion is nothing but moving the gaze from the bottom to the top. A simple movement of the eyes is enough.

"With the intensity of his spiritual life, Carlo fully and generously lived his fifteen years of life, leaving a profound impact on those who knew him. He was an expert with computers, he read books on computer engineering and left everyone in awe, but he put his gift at the service of others and used it to help his friends," Carlos mother said.[2]

THE TEXTURE OF HIS SPIRITUAL LIFE AND DEVOTIONS

Holiness was its true goal, but not just for him alone. To all, he gave his **toolkit for sainthood**: daily Mass, Communion, Rosary, Scripture, Eucharistic adoration, weekly Confession, and the willingness to give up something for others. Carlo also regularly offered up his sacrifices and prayed for the reparation of sins and offenses committed against the Sacred Heart of Jesus, which he felt alive and throbbing in the consecrated Host.

Carlo often prayed for the Pope, then John Paul II, and with a degree of passion that astonished his parish priest. Those who met the young man were left with an indelible impression that Jesus is, as ever was, the only One who can satisfy the heart of man.

It is impossible to talk about Carlo without mentioning his strong devotion to the Blessed Mother. He was fascinated by the apparitions in Lourdes and Fatima, and often spoke about Saint Bernadette Soubirous and the Little Shepherds of Fatima. Our Lady's messages of conversion, penance, and prayer - all this was lived concretely in his daily life. In a world hardened against the great truths of the Faith, Carlo shook consciences and invited us to look toward Heaven. In the family, in the school, in the midst of society, Carlo was a witness to eternity.

To quote Carlo: "Our aim has to be the infinite and not the finite. The Infinite is our homeland. We have always been expected in Heaven." [3]

A MISSIONARY OF NEW MEDIA

Carlo created several notable websites, one dedicated to young saints. He had a keen interest in those who were able to achieve holiness quickly. The website even included included a section where one could discover how many friends they had in heaven. Such an affable young man, he found friends *even in Heaven.*

Carlo demonstrated an amazing zeal and maturity for missionary work given his age, possibly due to another of his great friends in Heaven ...

Carlo's efforts were that of a true missionary: to reach as many people as possible and to introduce them to the beauty and joy of friendship with Jesus. Carlo took as his model St. Paul, the Apostle to the Gentiles, who committed himself to bring the Gospel to every corner of the globe even to the point of martyrdom.

Carlo was inspired by the works of fellow Italian <u>Blessed James Alberione</u>, who was himself also inspired by the Apostle Paul. Blessed James was the Founder of the Paulines and the Daughters of St. Paul. Both Blessed James and the religious societies he founded are recognized for putting new forms of media at the service of the Gospel.

THE EUCHARIST

Carlo maintained his curiosity without succumbing to mainstream interests: **"All people are born as originals but many die as photocopies."** To move towards this destination and not "die as photocopies," Carlo said that our compass has to be the Word of God. The Eucharist was his true north. Carlo put the Sacrament of the Eucharist at the center of his life and he called it "my highway to heaven." [3]

In 2002, Carlo accompanied his parents to listen to a priest friend speak at a presentation of the Little Eucharistic Catechism. He was fascinated by what he learned.

Carlo had an idea ...

He would create an exhibition on Eucharistic miracles. He said, "They must be able to see." Carlo wanted people to understand that Christ is truly present in the Eucharist by showing the moments throughout history when the Eucharist *visibly* became flesh and blood.

This was the confluence of all of Carlo's great loves: He wanted people to encounter the Eucharist and be reconciled to God by renewing the Miracle of the True Prescence. Carlo wanted to show people that the Eucharist *truly* is his great friend, Jesus.

Carlo immediately set to work by documenting the Eucharist miracles himself. He began dragging his parents across Europe to gather photographs of the miracles, themselves.

After two and a half years, the exhibition was ready. He had cataloged all the Eucharistic miracles *in world history*. Immediately, dioceses across the world began requesting the exhibit (www.miracolieucaristici.org).

Carlo had researched over "136 Eucharistic miracles that occurred over the centuries in different countries around the world, and have been acknowledged by the Church" and collected them into a virtual museum.[4] He created not only a website to house this virtual museum, but panel presentations, as well, that have traveled around the world.

According to the introductory panel, "In the United States alone, thanks to assistance from the Knights of Columbus, The Cardinal Newman Society and The Real Presence Association, with the support of Cardinal Raymond L. Burke, it has been hosted in thousands of parishes and more than 100 universities."

Carlo's exhibit soon crisscrossed the globe. It would reach all the places that he would never get to visit *in life*.

A DEATH TOO SOON

In early October 2006, Carlo fell ill. He had just completed a video, a labor of love, with the students of the Leo XIII high school. A few days later, he was being wheeled into the hospital of San Gerardo in Monza, Italy, a hospital founded by Saint Gerard, himself.

Carlo soon received his diagnosis ...

Crossing the threshold of the hospital, Carlo said to his mother: "From here I do not go out anymore!"

The diagnosis was acute promyelocytic leukemia. A few days earlier, Carlo told his parents: "I offer what I will have to suffer to the Lord for the Pope and for the Church, to skip Purgatory and go straight to Heaven."

Shortly after receiving his diagnosis, Carlo died on October 12, 2006. He died with a radiant smile on his face and offering his life for the Pope and for the Church.

He was buried in Assisi, the city of Saint Francis. On the day of his funeral, the church and the churchyard was flooded with his many friends and admirers. His mother describes the scene: "I have never seen people like this before." People filled the grieving mother's ears with stories about what Carlo had done, stories she had never heard.

THE IMPACT OF A LIFE

Having already reached so many through his international exhibit and internet ministry, Carlo's death had an immediate impact. Thousands of letters and emails reached the family.

Carlo's exhibit of Eucharistic miracles has reached the ends of the earth many times over, presented in Russia, Latin America, and even China. In the United States, thanks to the help of the Knights of Columbus, it has been hosted by thousands of parishes and hundreds of universities.

What was so special about Carlo?

He welcomed and loved Jesus as a friend, while still living deeply immersed in the world of today, mastering computer programming, film editing, website creation, and even editing comics by the age of 15. Despite being immersed in media so fraught with temptation, the Gospel thrived at his touch and to such an extent that he will probably become the Patron of the Internet.

Carlo remains an inspiration, especially to teenagers who struggle to be both holy and "normal," while remaining unique as an individual.

Carlo wrote that "We are all born as originals, but many die as photocopies." He survived the Xerox machine of modernity and the internet and actually thrived within it. In doing so, he showed each of us the path forward, giving us a means to navigate: **Our Compass**, he said, has to be the Word of God, which we have to keep constantly before us. Also, **"Our Goal must be the infinite, not the finite. The Infinite is our homeland. We have always been expected in Heaven."**

Just after five years of canonical norms, the Diocese of Milan immediately started the process of beatification. On Thursday, November 24, 2016, Cardinal Angelo Scola closed the diocesesan phase in the canonization process.[4] The next stage in the canonization process is to send all the biographical works accumulated, perhaps even this one, to Rome to be reviewed by the Congregation for the Causes of the Saints. If approved, the cause for Carlo Acutis will proceed and the Holy Father can declare him "Venerable."

If you encounter any miracles due to Carlo's intercession or if you can share stories of his impact, especially on youth, please contact share at http://carloacutis.com.

Please also remember to share the story of this amazing young man!

[1] "The Saint of the Month: Blessed Carlo Acutis, possible future patron of the web," Parrocchia Santa Maria Assunta

[2] "Italy moved by teen who offers life for the Church and the Pope," Catholic News Agency, Oct 24, 2007.

[3] "Biography," The Carlo Acutis Association and the Cause of Beatification of the Servant of God Carlo Acutis, official website.

[4] "Computer geek" takes one more step toward sainthood," by Philip Kosloski, Dec 3, 2016.

- The Official website of the CARLO ACUTIS Association and the Cause of Beatification of the Servant of God Carlo Acutis, "Biography"

CPSIA information can be obtained
at www.ICGtesting.com
Printed in the USA
LVHW100021050919
629919LV00047BA/881/P